The MAILBOX®
The Education Center®

S0-AHR-653

Everything Science

Timesaving tools for 22 popular science topics

- **Animals**
- **Caring for the earth**
- **Rocks and soil**
- **Weather**
- **Magnets**
- **Plants**

- **Solids and liquids**
- **Seasons**
- **Bugs**
- **Sink or float**

Plus many more!

Managing Editor: Kelly Robertson

Editorial Team: Becky S. Andrews, Diane Badden, Kimberley Bruck, Karen A. Brudnak, Kimberly Brugger-Murphy, Pam Crane, Sarah Foreman, Pierce Foster, Tazmen Hansen, Marsha Heim, Lori Z. Henry, Lucia Kemp Henry, Debra Liverman, Kitty Lowrance, Brenda Miner, Jennifer Nunn, Gerri Primak, Mark Rainey, Greg D. Rieves, Hope Rodgers, Eliseo De Jesus Santos II, Donna K. Teal, Rachael Traylor, Sharon M. Tresino

www.themailbox.com

What's

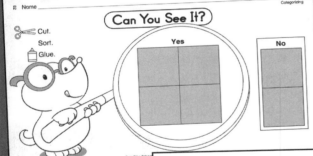

Magnets

Caring for the Earth

Living and Nonliving

topic-based coloring pages

fun practice pages

Can You See It?

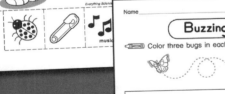

Buzzing Along

A Happy Hiker

Inside

picture cards

sorting mats

Which Bush?

Time to Hatch!

fold-and-go booklets

food,

exercise,

My Body Needs...

z z z

and sleep.

Plus more than 20 additional ways to use the teaching tools for select topics!

Table of Contents

Size and Shape

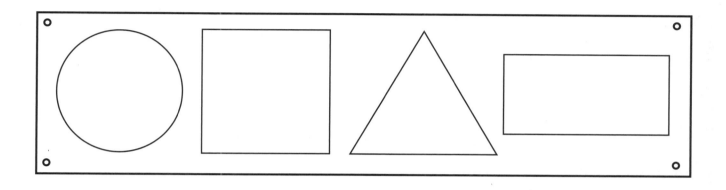

Note to the teacher: Ask a child to color the picture. As she works, assess her prior knowledge by asking her to name the shapes at the top of the page. Then have her name other shapes she sees on her paper and the objects that contain them *(triangle-shaped block, circle-shaped wheels, rectangle-shaped toy box).* Ask questions such as "If the wheels were square, would the truck roll?" or "Would a block fit in the dump truck?" to reinforce that an object's shape or size may be important to its function.

Why?

Which bear will fit?

Why?

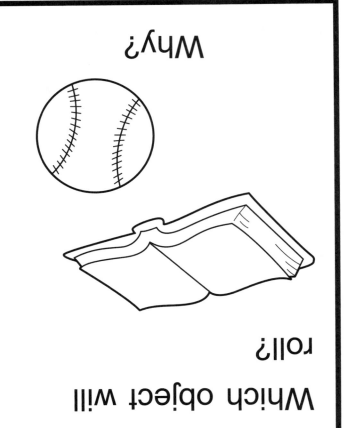

Which object will roll?

Where does the peg go?

Why?

Size and Shape

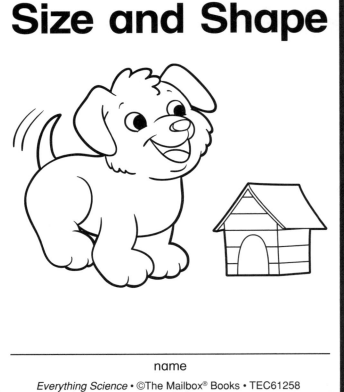

name

Everything Science • ©The Mailbox® Books • TEC61258

Fold-and-Go Booklet: To make a booklet, cut on the bold line. Fold along the thin horizontal line (keeping the programming to the outside) and then fold along the thin vertical line (keeping the cover to the outside). Read each booklet page aloud and have a child color the correct answer. Have him explain each answer, encouraging him to use words such as *round, flat, big, small,* and *square.*

Name_____

Listen and Do

Draw.

Everything Science • ©The Mailbox® Books • TEC61258

Size and Shape

A _____ is _____

than me and is shaped like a _____.

by _____
name

Everything Science • ©The Mailbox® Books • TEC61258

Class Book Page: Have a child write her name on a copy of the page and think of an object. Then have her determine whether the object is bigger or smaller than her, as well as what the object is shaped like. She dictates or writes words to complete the sentence and then illustrates her work. Publish the pages in a class book titled "Different Sizes and Shapes!"

Name_____

Party Time!

Listen.
Color.

Celebrate!

Note to the teacher: Give students the following directions: First, color two same-size circle-shaped objects green. Then find the two triangle-shaped objects and color the larger one purple. Next, color the smaller triangle-shaped object yellow. After that, find the two square-shaped objects and color the larger one orange. Then color the smaller one red. Finally, color a long rectangle-shaped object blue.

10 Name

Shapely Things

✂ Cut.

🖊 Glue to match.

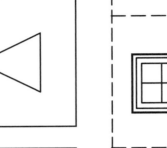
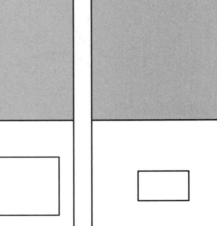

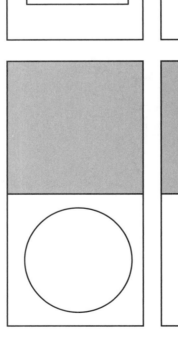

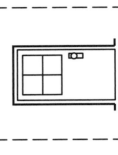
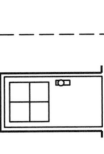

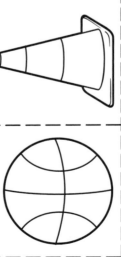

Everything Science • ©The Mailbox® Books • TEC61258

Note to the teacher: Have a child cut out the cards at the bottom of the page. Then have him glue each card to a box to match its size and shape.

Weight

Note to the teacher: Ask a child to color the picture. As the child works, assess his prior knowledge by asking him to name a picture on his paper of something that is heavy *(hippo, rock)* or something that is light *(kite, butterfly)*.

Which weighs **less?**

Which weighs **more?**

Do the bears weigh the **same?**
Yes or **No**

Weight

How do you know?

name

Everything Science • ©The Mailbox® Books • TEC61258

Fold-and-Go Booklet: To make a booklet, cut on the bold line. Fold along the thin horizontal line (keeping the programming to the outside) and then fold along the thin vertical line (keeping the cover to the outside). Read each booklet page aloud and have a child circle the correct answer. For the final booklet page, have each child explain her answer.

Listen and Do

Draw.

Everything Science • ©The Mailbox® Books • TEC61258

Note to the teacher: Provide oral directions, such as "Circle an instrument that is too heavy to pick up" or "Color an object that is light enough to float in the air." Then specify what you would like the child to draw in the empty box, saying, for example, "Draw something in the classroom that is light enough for you to pick up."

Weight

Some things are heavy, like _____.

Some things are light, like _____.

by _____
name

Class Book Page: Have a child write her name on a copy of the page and then dictate or write a response. If a child seems uncertain how to complete the prompts, suggest objects that are heavy and light for her to choose from. Then have her illustrate her work. Publish the pages in a class book titled "Heavy and Light."

Name _____

A Heavy Load

Color the item in each box that weighs more.

Name

16

Cut.

Sort.

Glue.

Moving Day

Light

Heavy

Sink or Float

Everything Science • ©The Mailbox® Books • TEC61258

Note to the teacher: Ask a child to color the picture. As the child works, assess her prior knowledge by asking her to name something on her paper that sinks *(anchor, shell, rock)* or floats *(boat, buoy)*.

Does a key

sink or **float?**

Does a ball

sink or **float?**

Does a rock
sink or **float?**

Sink or Float?

name

Everything Science • ©The Mailbox® Books • TEC61258

Fold-and-Go Booklet: To make a booklet, cut on the bold line. Fold along the thin horizontal line (keeping the programming to the outside) and then fold along the thin vertical line (keeping the cover to the outside). To use the booklet, read aloud each page and have students circle either *sink* or *float*.

Name _____

Listen and Do

Draw.

Everything Science • ©The Mailbox® Books • TEC61258

Note to the teacher: Provide oral directions, such as "Circle a coin that sinks in water" or "Color a round object that floats in water." Then specify what you would like the child to draw in the empty box, saying, for example, "Draw an object found at your home that sinks in water."

Sink or Float

Some things sink like _____.

Some things float like _____.

by _____
name

Class Book Page: Have a child write his name on a copy of the page and then dictate or write a response. If a child seems uncertain how to complete the prompts, suggest different objects that sink and float for him to choose from. Then have him illustrate his work. Publish the pages in a class book titled "Some Things Sink, and Some Things Float!"

20

Name_____

Floaters and Sinkers

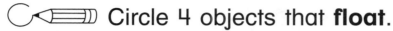 Circle 4 objects that **float**.

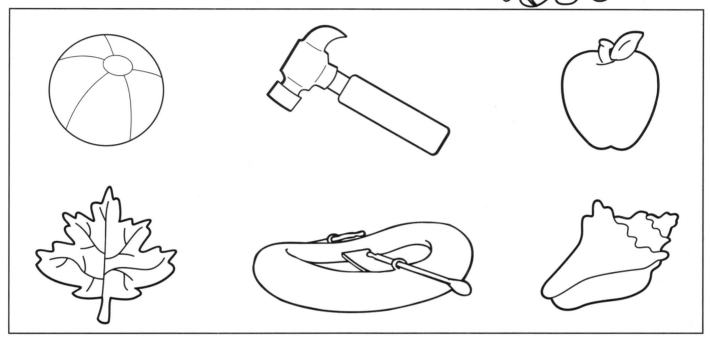

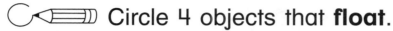 Circle 4 objects that **sink**.

What Sinks? What Floats?

 Cut.

Sort.

 Glue.

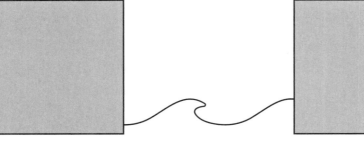

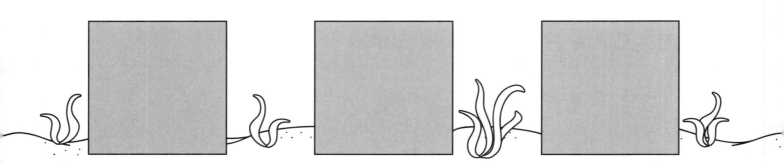

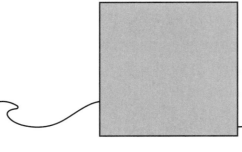

Everything Science • ©The Mailbox® Books • TEC61258

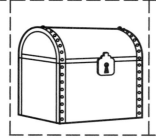 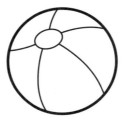   

Temperature

Everything Science • ©The Mailbox® Books • TEC61258

Note to the teacher: Ask a child to color the picture. As the child works, assess his prior knowledge by asking him to name a picture on his paper of something that is hot *(stove, oven, pie, pot)* or cold *(drink, pitcher, ice cubes, snow)*.

23

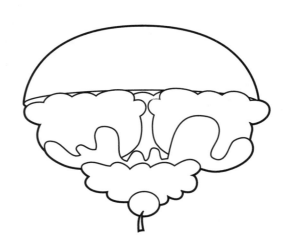

Is ice cream
hot or cold?

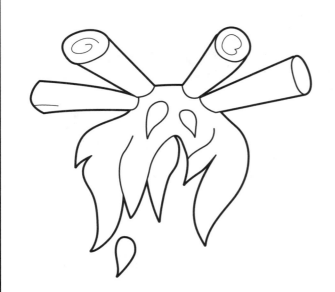

Is a fire
hot or cold?

Is snow
hot or cold?

Temperature

_____
name

Fold-and-Go Booklet: To make a booklet, cut on the bold line. Fold along the thin horizontal line (keeping the programming to the outside) and then fold along the thin vertical line (keeping the cover to the outside). To use the booklet, read each booklet page aloud and have students circle the correct answer.

Listen and Do

Draw.

Note to the teacher: Provide oral directions, such as "Color a picture of something you wear when it's cold outside" or "Circle an object you put in a drink to make it cold." Then specify what you would like the child to draw in the empty box, saying, for example, "Draw a picture of your favorite hot food."

Temperature

Some things are hot, like _____.

Some things are cold, like _____.

by _____
name

Class Book Page: Have a child write her name on a copy of the page and then dictate or write a response. If a child seems uncertain how to complete the prompts, suggest different things that are hot and cold for her to choose from. Then have her illustrate her work. Publish the pages in a class book titled "Hot or Cold?"

Name_____

Hot and Cold

🖍 Color four objects that are hot.

🖍 Color four objects that are cold.

Where Does It Belong?

Cut.

Sort.

Glue.

350°

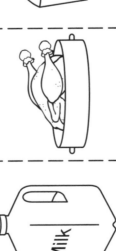

Milk

Everything Science • ©The Mailbox® Books • TEC61258

Magnets

Note to the teacher: Ask a child to color the picture. As the child works, assess her prior knowledge by asking her to name a picture on her paper of something that a magnet would be attracted to *(nail, paper clip, safety pin)* or would not be attracted to *(disposable cup, banana, crayon).*   29

No!

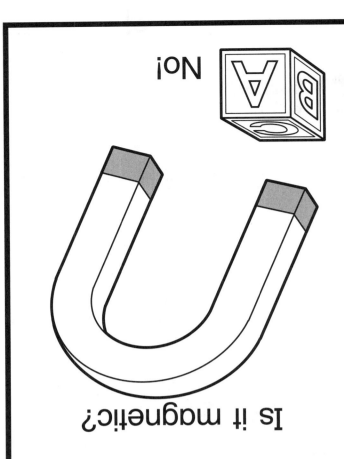

Is it magnetic?

Yes!

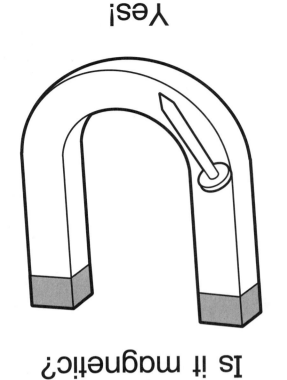

Is it magnetic?

Is it magnetic?

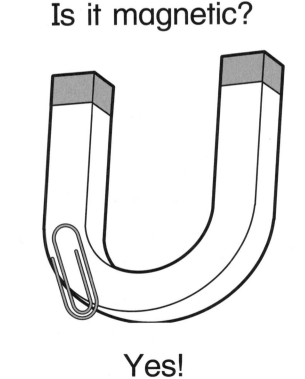

Yes!

Magnets

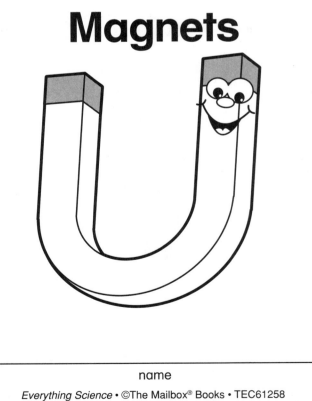

_____
name

Fold-and-Go Booklet: To make a booklet, cut on the bold line. Fold along the thin horizontal line (keeping the programming to the outside) and then fold along the thin vertical line (keeping the cover to the outside). Read each booklet page aloud. After reading the booklet, ask a child to explain why magnets attract some objects and not others.

30

Name_____

Listen and Do

Draw.

Everything Science • ©The Mailbox® Books • TEC61258

Note to the teacher: Provide oral directions, such as "Circle an object that is magnetic and keeps food cold" or "Cross off an object that is not magnetic and is used to dry off with after a bath." Then specify what you would like the child to draw in the empty box, saying, for example, "Draw a picture of something shiny that is magnetic."

Magnets

A _____ is magnetic.

A _____ is not magnetic.

by _____
name

Class Book Page: Have a child write his name on a copy of the page and then dictate or write a response. If a child seems uncertain how to complete the prompts, have him use a magnet to find objects in the classroom that the magnet is and is not attracted to. Then have him illustrate his work. Publish the pages in a class book titled "Magnets Are Magnificent!"

Name _____

Mouse's Magnet

Is it magnetic?

 Color 😊 or 🙁 to show your answer.

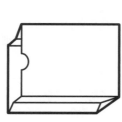

😊 Yes   🙁 No

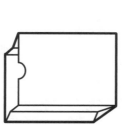

😊 Yes   🙁 No

😊 Yes   🙁 No

🙁 No

😊 Yes

🙁 No

😊 Yes

🙁 No

😊 Yes

33

Name _____

Is It Magnetic?

Cut. Sort.

Glue.

Yes

No

Solids and Liquids

Everything Science • ©The Mailbox® Books • TEC61258

Note to the teacher: Ask a child to color the picture. As the child works, assess his prior knowledge by asking him to name a picture on his paper of something that is a solid *(rock, log)* or something that is a liquid *(rain, puddle).*

Some things are
liquids.

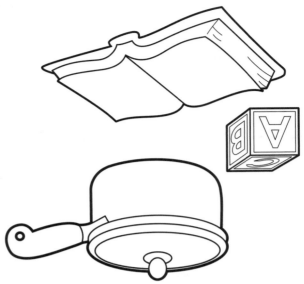

Some things are
solids.

Some things change
from a **solid** to
a **liquid.**

Do you know why?

Solids and
Liquids

_____
name

Everything Science • ©The Mailbox® Books • TEC61258

Fold-and-Go Booklet: To make a booklet, cut on the bold line. Fold along the thin horizontal line (keeping the programming to the outside) and then fold along the thin vertical line (keeping the cover to the outside). Read each booklet page aloud. For the final page, ask the child to explain why some objects change from a solid to a liquid.

Name_____

Listen and Do

Draw.

Note to the teacher: Provide oral directions, such as "Circle a picture of a solid object used for cooking" or "Color a picture of a liquid used for hand washing." Then specify what you would like the child to draw in the empty box, saying, for example, "Draw a picture of something in the classroom that is a solid."

Solids and Liquids

Some things are solids, like _____.

Some things are liquids, like _____.

by _____
name

Solid or Liquid?

Circle 4 pictures of solids.

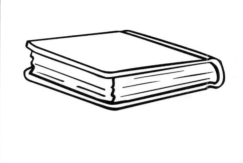

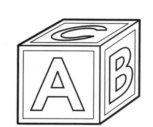

Circle 4 pictures of liquids.

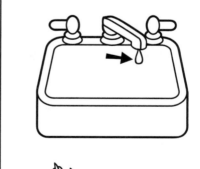

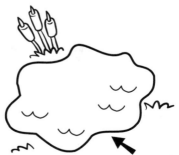

Name _____

Which Is It?

Cut.
Sort.
Glue.

Solid

Liquid

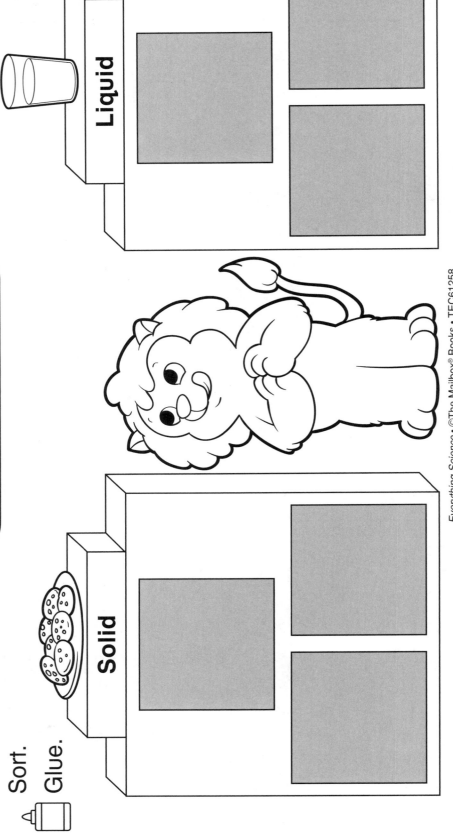

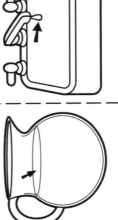
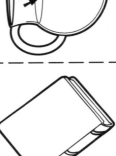

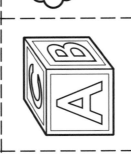

Everything Science • ©The Mailbox® Books • TEC61258

Living and Nonliving

Note to the teacher: Ask each child to color the picture. As the child works, assess his prior knowledge by asking him to name a picture on his paper of something that is living *(tree, deer, flowers)* or is nonliving *(rocks)*.

41

Picture Cards: Living and Nonliving

TEC61258

TEC61258

TEC61258

TEC61258

TEC61258

TEC61258

TEC61258

TEC61258

TEC61258

Everything Science • ©The Mailbox® Books • TEC61258

Which Barrel?

Everything Science • ©The Mailbox® Books • TEC61258

Sorting Mat: Have students sort magazine pictures showing living and nonliving things or sort the picture cards from page 42. A student also may use an ink pad and assorted rubber stamps to stamp the barrels with images of living and nonliving things.

No!

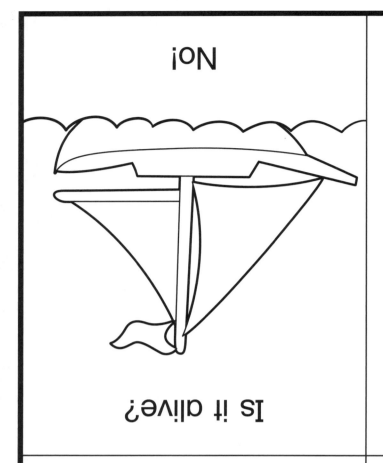

Is it alive?

Yes!

Is it alive?

How do you know?

Living and Nonliving

name

Everything Science • ©The Mailbox® Books • TEC61258

Fold-and-Go Booklet: To make a booklet, cut on the bold line. Fold along the thin horizontal line (keeping the programming to the outside) and then fold along the thin vertical line (keeping the cover to the outside). For the final booklet page, have the child explain how she knows a duck is alive and a boat is not.

Name_____

Listen and Do

Draw.

Note to the teacher: Provide oral directions, such as "Circle a nonliving object that can be worn" or "Color a living thing that lives in water."
Then specify what you would like the child to draw in the empty box by saying, for example, "Draw something from the classroom that is alive." 45

Living and Nonliving

_____ knows living things

name

Class Book Page: Have a child write her name on a copy of the page and then dictate or write a response. If a child seems uncertain how to complete the prompt, suggest different verbs to continue the sentence, such as *are, need, live,* and *grow.* Then have her illustrate her work. Publish the pages in a class book titled "We Have Learned a Lot About Living Things!"

Name_____

Lots of Living Things

Circle 3 pictures of living things in each row.

Name

48

On the Farm

✂ Cut.

Glue 4 living things on the farm.

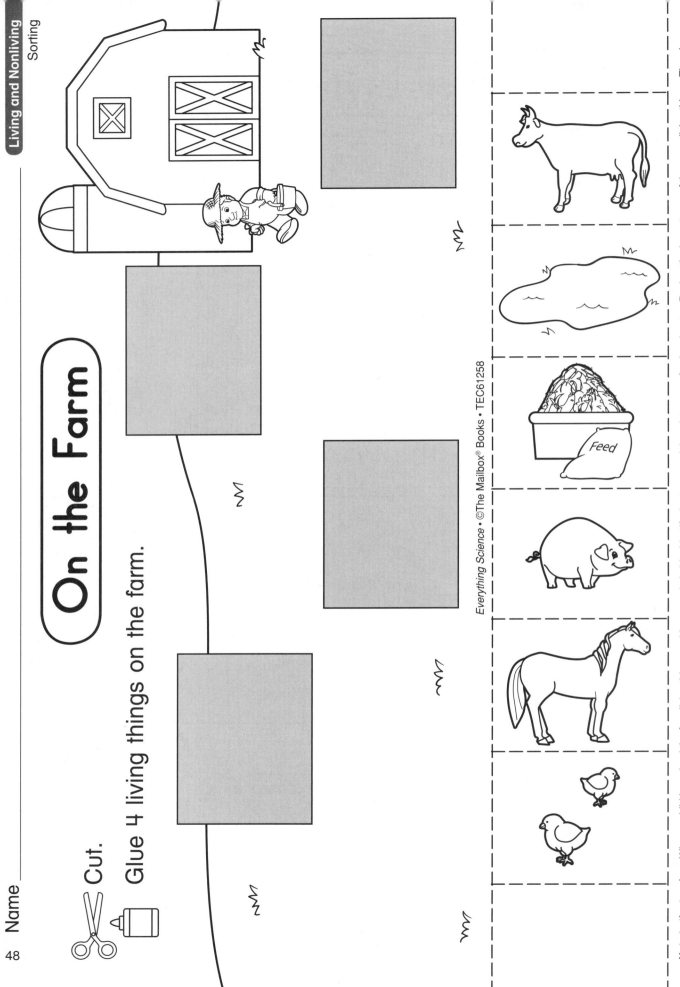

Everything Science • ©The Mailbox® Books • TEC61258

Feed

Note to the teacher: When a child has glued the four living things on his paper, help him identify the two remaining pictures as food and water. Review the importance of these nonliving things. Then have him glue the two pictures on his paper and underline them to distinguish them from the living things.

My Body

Note to the teacher: Have the child color the picture. As the child works, encourage him to point to and name body parts on the featured youngsters.

Picture Cards: Body Parts

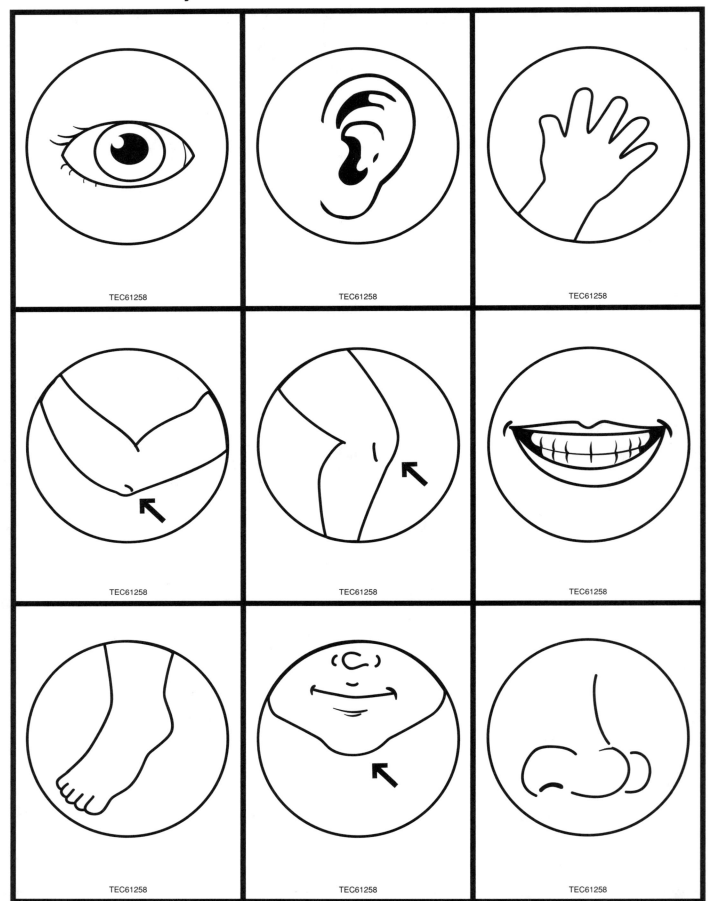

TEC61258

TEC61258

TEC61258

TEC61258

TEC61258

TEC61258

TEC61258

TEC61258

TEC61258

Everything Science • ©The Mailbox® Books • TEC61258

Body Match

Everything Science • ©The Mailbox® Books • TEC61258

Matching Mat: Have youngsters match the picture cards from page 50 to the corresponding body parts on the mat. As an alternative, have students cut pictures of body parts from magazines and place them on the mat.

51

exercise,

food.

and sleep.

My Body Needs...

_____
name

Everything Science • ©The Mailbox® Books • TEC61258

Fold-and-Go Booklet: To make a booklet, cut on the bold line. Fold along the thin horizontal line (keeping the programming to the outside) and then fold along the thin vertical line (keeping the cover to the outside). Have students color the pages and identify three important things their bodies need.

52

Listen and Do

Draw.

Note to the teacher: Provide oral directions, such as "Circle a drink that is not a healthy choice for your body" or "Color a purple fruit that is healthy for your body." Then specify what you would like the child to draw in the empty box, saying, for example, "Draw a food that is healthy for your body."

My Body

_____'s body can
name

_____.

Class Book Page: Have a child write her name on a copy of the page and then write or dictate a response. If a child seems uncertain how to complete the prompt, suggest activities such as running, jumping, or skating. Then have her illustrate her work. Publish the pages in a class book titled "What Can Our Bodies Do?"

Two for You!

Color the body parts that you have 2 of.

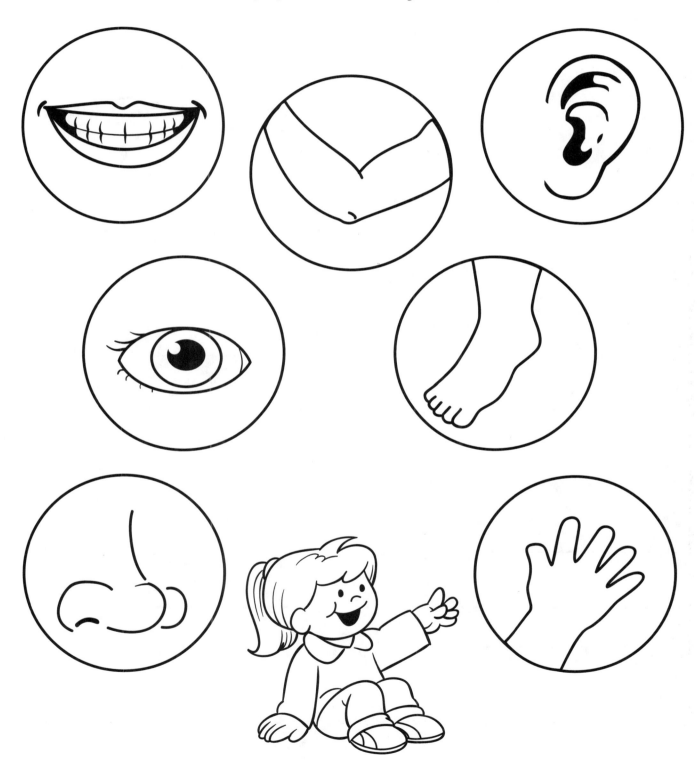

A Friendly Face

✂ Cut.

🖋 Glue to match.

| mouth | hair | chin |
| eye | ear | nose |

Sight

Everything Science • ©The Mailbox® Books • TEC61258

Note to the teacher: Ask a child to color the picture. As the child works, assess his prior knowledge by asking him to name something on his paper for which he uses his sense of sight *(looking at a clock, looking at a calendar, building with blocks)* or does not use his sense of sight *(listening to music).*

Yes!

a bird

I can see…

Yes!

a flag

I can see…

I can see…

music

No!

Why not?

Sight

name

Everything Science • ©The Mailbox® Books • TEC61258

Fold-and-Go Booklet: To make a booklet, cut on the bold line. Fold along the thin horizontal line (keeping the programming to the outside) and then fold along the thin vertical line (keeping the cover to the outside). For the final page, have the child explain why she cannot see music.

Name _____

Listen and Do

wind

August

S	M	T	W	T	F	S
						1
2	3	4	5	6	7	8
9	10	11	12	13	14	15
16	17	18	19	20	21	22
23 30	24 31	25	26	27	28	29

Draw.

Note to the teacher: Provide oral directions, such as "Color an object you look at to tell the time" or "Circle something you can feel and hear but cannot see." Then specify what you would like the child to draw in the empty box, saying, for example, "Draw your favorite thing to do that uses your sense of sight."

Sight

I use my sense of sight to _____.

by _____
name

Class Book Page: Have a child write his name on a copy of the page and then write or dictate a response. If a child seems uncertain how to complete the prompt, suggest different things he uses his sense of sight for. Then have him illustrate his work. Publish the pages in a class

book titled "So Much to See!"

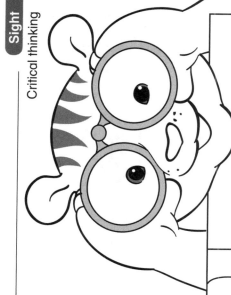

Look at That!

Circle the pictures that show things Tiger uses

 his 👁 👁 for.

The Case of the Missing Stripes

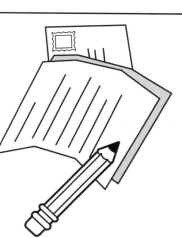

Name _____

62

Can You See It?

Cut.

Sort.

Glue.

Yes

No

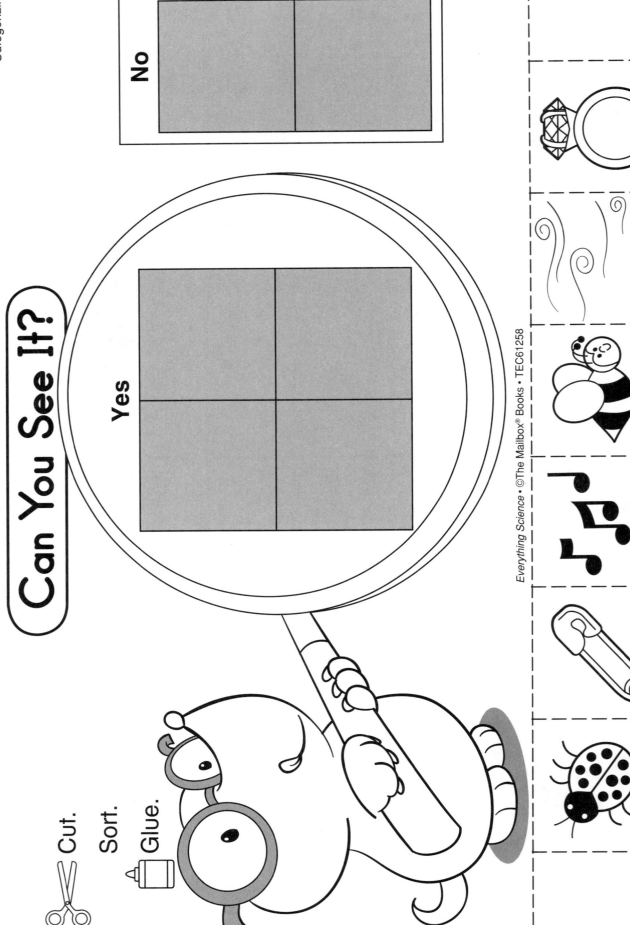

wind

music

Sound

Everything Science • ©The Mailbox® Books • TEC61258

Note to the teacher: Ask a child to color the picture. As the child works, assess her prior knowledge by asking her to name a picture of something on her paper that can make a sound *(alarm clock, vacuum, telephone)* or that cannot make a sound *(teddy bear, rug, dresser, nightstand)*.

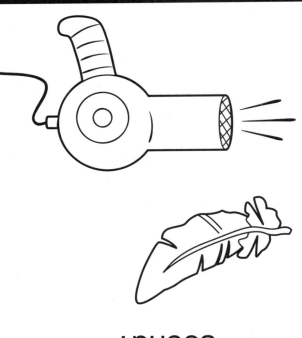

Which makes a
sound?

Which sound is
louder?

Buzz!

Which sound is softer?

CHIRP!

ROAR!

Sound

_____
name

Fold-and-Go Booklet: To make a booklet, cut on the bold line. Fold along the thin horizontal line (keeping the programming to the outside) and then fold along the thin vertical line (keeping the cover to the outside). Read each booklet page aloud and have each child circle the correct answer.

Listen and Do

Draw.

Everything Science • ©The Mailbox® Books • TEC61258

Note to the teacher: Provide oral directions, such as "Circle an animal that makes a barking sound" or "Color an emergency vehicle that has a loud siren." Then specify what you would like the child to draw in the empty box, saying, for example, "Draw something that makes a loud sound."

Sound

I can hear _____.

by _____
名 name

Class Book Page: Have a child write his name on a copy of the page and then dictate or write a response. If a child seems uncertain how to complete the prompt, suggest different things he can hear. Then have him illustrate his work. Publish the pages in a class book titled "Sounds Are All Around!"

What Makes Noise?

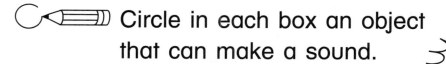 Circle in each box an object that can make a sound.

  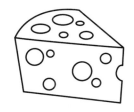

 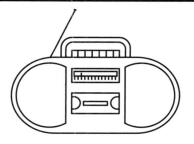 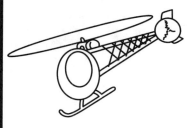 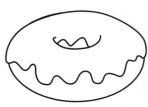

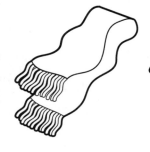 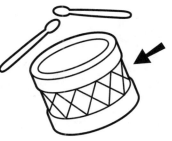  

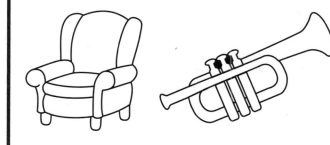  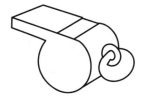

Name _____

68

Can You Hear It?

Cut. Sort.

Glue.

Yes

No

Everything Science • ©The Mailbox® Books • TEC61258

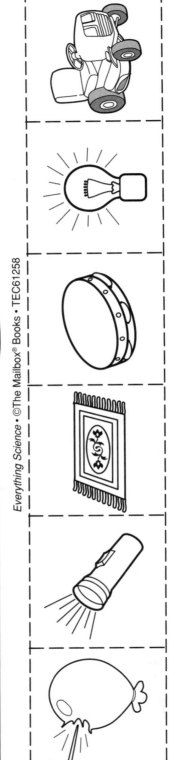

Taste

Everything Science • ©The Mailbox® Books • TEC61258

69

sour.

Some foods taste

sweet.

Some foods taste

Some foods taste **salty.**

Taste

name

Everything Science • ©The Mailbox® Books • TEC61258

Fold-and-Go Booklet: To make a booklet, cut on the bold line. Fold along the thin horizontal line (keeping the programming to the outside) and then fold along the thin vertical line (keeping the cover to the outside). Read each booklet page aloud and have each child circle on the page the food with the corresponding taste.

Listen and Do

Draw.

Note to the teacher: Provide oral directions, such as "Color a treat that tastes sweet and melts while you eat it" or "Cross off a fruit that is yellow and tastes sour." Then specify what you would like the child to draw in the empty box, saying, for example, "Draw something you like to eat that tastes sweet."

71

Taste

I like to eat _____.
                        food

_____ tastes
        food

_____.
salty, sour, sweet

by _____
              name

Class Book Page: Have a child write his name on a copy of the page and then dictate or write a response. If a child seems uncertain how to complete the prompt, suggest different sweet, salty, and sour foods for him to choose from. Then have him illustrate his work. Publish the pages in a class book titled "Tasty Treats!"

72

Fabulous Food

Follow the directions in each box.

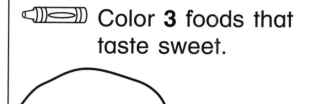 Color **3** foods that taste sweet.

Circle **3** foods that taste salty.

Cross out **2** foods that taste sour.

Name _____

How Does It Taste?

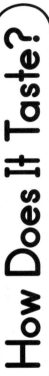

Cut.

Sort.

Glue.

Sweet 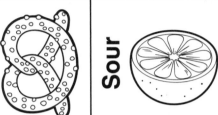		
Salty 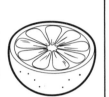		
Sour		

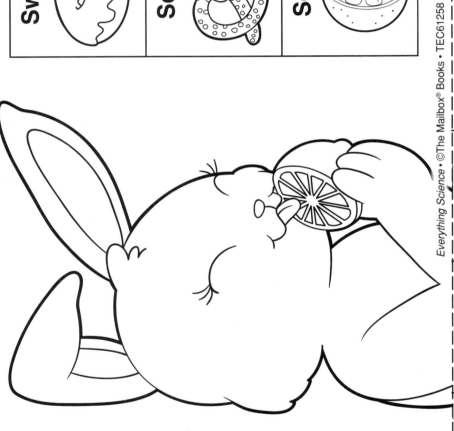

Everything Science • ©The Mailbox® Books • TEC61258

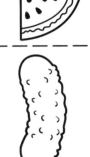
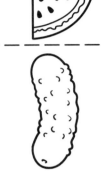

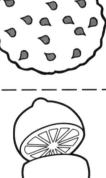

74

Touch

Note to the teacher: Ask a child to color the picture. As the child works, assess her prior knowledge by asking her to name a picture on her paper of things that are soft (*pillow, rabbit, blanket*) or hard (*bat, blocks, xylophone, mallets*).

75

block

Some things feel
hard.

teddy bear

Some things feel
soft.

Some things feel
smooth.

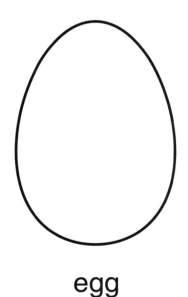

egg

Touch

_____
name

Everything Science • ©The Mailbox® Books • TEC61258

Fold-and-Go Booklet: To make a booklet, cut on the bold line. Fold along the thin horizontal line (keeping the programming to the outside) and then fold along the thin vertical line (keeping the cover to the outside). Read each booklet page aloud. After reading each page, invite youngsters to name objects that feel similar to the item on the page.

Listen and Do

Draw.

Everything Science • ©The Mailbox® Books • TEC61258

Note to the teacher: Provide oral directions, such as "Color something soft you lay your head on when you go to sleep" or "Circle something hard that is found in the ocean." Then specify what you would like the child to draw in the empty box, saying, for example, "Draw an object from your bedroom at home that feels soft."

Touch

When I touch _____,

it feels _____.

by _____
   name

Everything Science • ©The Mailbox® Books • TEC61258

Class Book Page: Have a child write her name on a copy of the page and then dictate or write a response. If a child seems uncertain how to complete the prompt, provide several objects with different textures for her to choose from. Then have her illustrate her work. Publish the pages in a class book titled "Touchable Textures."

Name _____

Things That Feel...

🖍 Color the items with a similar texture.

Soft	Rough	Smooth

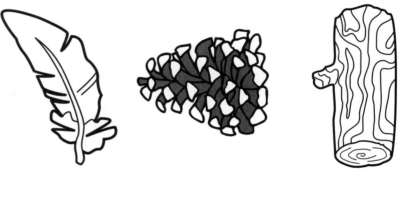

How Does It Feel?

 Cut.

Glue to match the texture.

Soft

Rough

Hard

Smell

Note to the teacher: Ask a child to color the picture. As the child works, assess his prior knowledge by asking him to name a picture on his paper of something that he can smell *(skunk, flowers, smoke)*.

I can smell…

I can smell…

I can smell…

Smell

_____
name

Everything Science • ©The Mailbox® Books • TEC61258

Fold-and-Go Booklet: To make a booklet, cut on the bold line. Fold along the thin horizontal line (keeping the programming to the outside) and then fold along the thin vertical line (keeping the cover to the outside). Read each booklet page aloud. After reading each page, have each child color the objects he can smell.

Listen and Do

Draw.

Everything Science • ©The Mailbox® Books • TEC61258

Note to the teacher: Provide oral directions, such as "Circle an animal that gives off a bad smell" or "Color something that you cannot smell that is used to hold flowers." Then specify what you would like the child to draw in the empty box, saying, for example, "Draw something that smells good that you like to eat."

Smell

I like to smell _____.

I do not like to smell _____.

by _____
name

Class Book Page: Have a child write her name on a copy of the page and then write or dictate a response. If a child seems uncertain how to complete the prompt, have her look through a magazine for ideas to choose from. Publish the pages in a class book titled "Good Smells and Bad Smells!"

What a Scent!

Circle in each row 3 pictures of things you can smell.

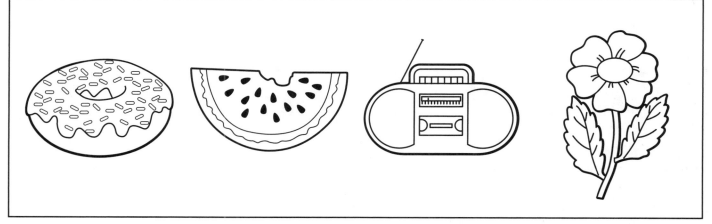

Name _____

86

Does It Have a Smell?

Cut.
Sort.
Glue.

Things that do not have a smell

Things that have a smell

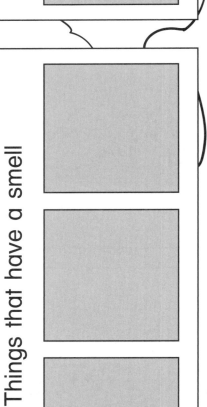

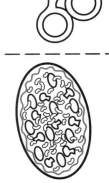

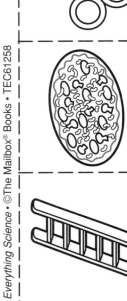

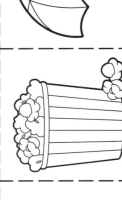

Animals

Everything Science • ©The Mailbox® Books • TEC61258

Note to the teacher: Ask each child to color the picture. As the child works, assess his prior knowledge by asking him the names of the animals on the page. Then encourage him to name animals that are not pictured.

TEC61258

TEC61258

TEC61258

TEC61258

TEC61258

TEC61258

TEC61258

TEC61258

Picture Cards: Set Two—Animal Coverings

TEC61258

TEC61258

TEC61258

TEC61258

TEC61258

TEC61258

TEC61258

TEC61258

TEC61258

Which Bush?

90

Sorting Mat: Have students sort magazine pictures of animals or sort the cards from page 89. A student may also attach animal stickers to the bushes, sorting big animals from small animals.

Everything Science • ©The Mailbox® Books • TEC61258

How are they
different?

**Animal
Differences**

_____
name

Everything Science • ©The Mailbox® Books • TEC61258

How are they
different?

How are they
different?

Fold-and-Go Booklet: To make a booklet, cut on the bold line. Fold along the thin horizontal line (keeping the programming to the outside) and then fold along the thin vertical line (keeping the cover to the outside). Read each page aloud and have students describe how the two animals pictured are different.

Name_____

Listen and Do

Draw.

Everything Science • ©The Mailbox® Books • TEC61258

Note to the teacher: Provide oral directions, such as "Circle the baby that's called a duckling" or "Color the mother of a fawn." Then specify what you would like the child to draw in the empty box, saying, for example, "Draw the mother of a puppy."

Animals

_____'s favorite animal
                    name

is _____ because

_____.

Class Book Page: Have a child write her name on a copy of the page and then write or dictate a response. Then have her illustrate her work. Publish the pages in a class book titled "Our Favorite Animals."

Name _____

Feeding Time!

✏ Draw a line to match each animal to its food.

Everything Science • ©The Mailbox® Books • TEC61258

Who Lives Here?

 Cut.

Glue each animal next to its home.

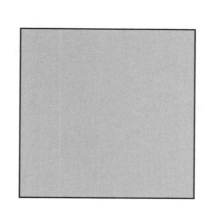

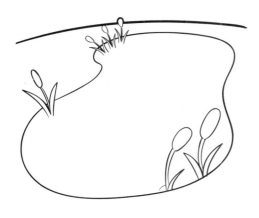

How Do They Move?

 Cut.

Glue to show how the animal moves.

Hop

Swim

Fly

Everything Science • ©The Mailbox® Books • TEC61258

Picture Cards: Set One
Page 88

Small group: Label a folded sheet of construction paper with the question shown. A youngster glues an animal home card below the question. Then she opens up the paper, glues on the appropriate animal card, and adds details as desired. Invite each student, in turn, to read the front of her paper and have classmates guess the animal. Then have her open her paper to reveal the animal.

Who Lives Here?

Picture Cards: Set Two
Page 89

Whole group: Place three plastic hoops on the floor and label the hoops as shown. Cut out a copy of the cards and place them in a bag. Have a child draw a card and name the animal. Encourage the remaining youngsters to identify whether the animal has fur, feathers, or scales. Then prompt the student to place the card in the appropriate hoop. Continue with the remaining cards.

Fur

Scales

Feathers

"Listen and Do"
Page 92

Center: Cut out the grid to make separate mother and baby animal cards. Label a sheet of construction paper "Mothers" and a second sheet "Babies." Then place the papers and cards at a center. A youngster names the animal on a card, identifies it as a mother or baby animal, and then places it on the corresponding sheet of paper. He continues until each card has been placed.

Class Book Page
Page 93

Individual: After students complete the prompt and illustration on the page, have each child share her work. Then collect the papers. At a later time, return each child's paper and encourage her to draw a picture of her least favorite animal on the back. Then have her dictate a sentence about this animal. If desired, have each student share her drawing with the class.

Sarah's least favorite animal is a lion because lions can be scary.

Plants

Note to the teacher: Ask each child to color the picture. As the child works, assess her prior knowledge by asking her to name a picture on her paper of something that is a plant *(flower, tree, bush)* or something that is not a plant *(cat, bumblebee, sun)*.

Picture Cards: Set One—Plants

TEC61258

TEC61258

TEC61258

TEC61258

TEC61258

TEC61258

Distracter Cards

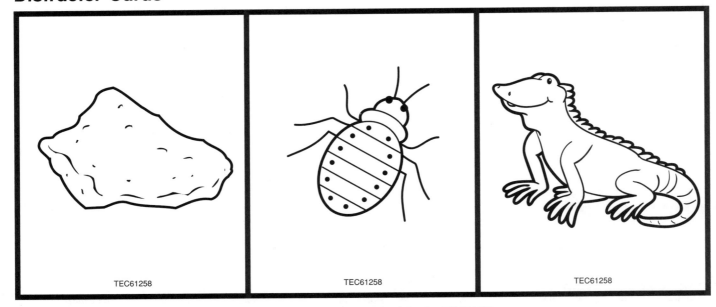

TEC61258

TEC61258

TEC61258

Picture Cards: Set Two—Plant Parts

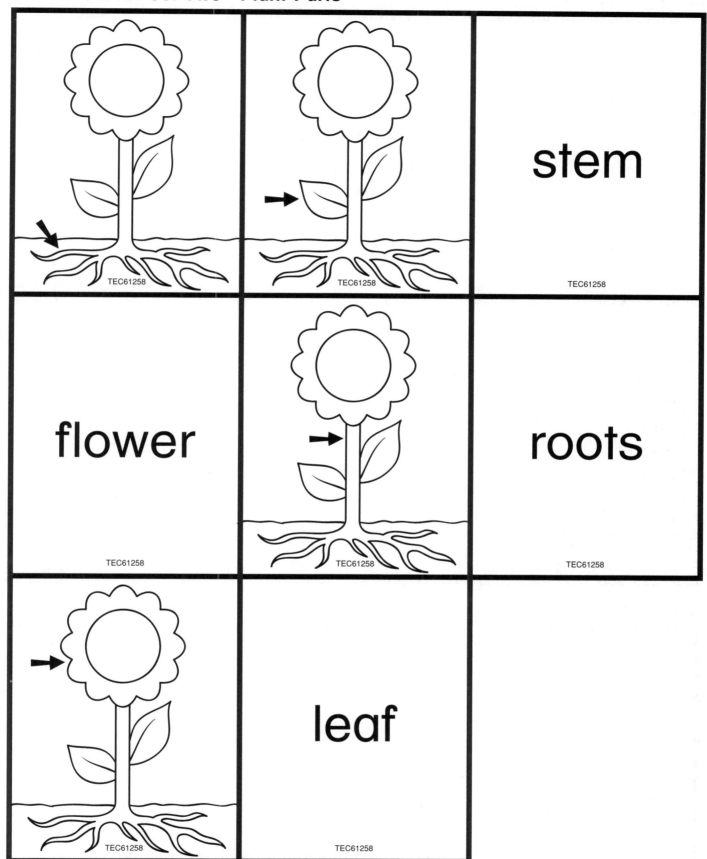

stem

flower

roots

leaf

TEC61258

Which Pot?

Everything Science • ©The Mailbox® Books • TEC61258

Sorting Mat: Have students sort magazine pictures of different types of plants or sort the picture cards from page 100.

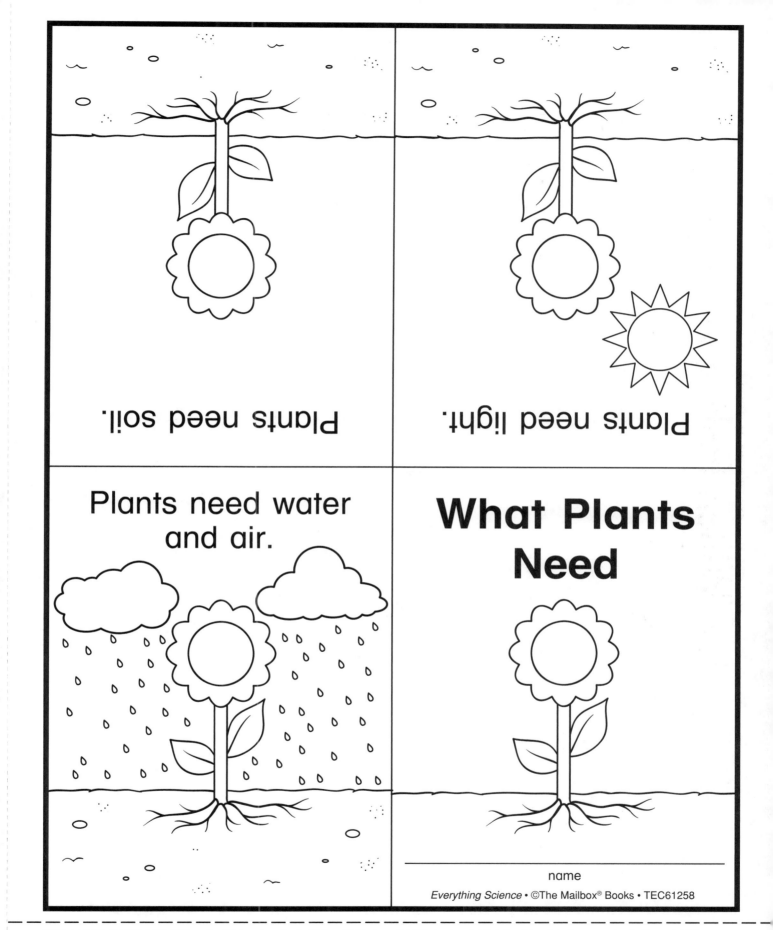

Plants need soil.

Plants need light.

Plants need water
and air.

What Plants Need

name

Everything Science • ©The Mailbox® Books • TEC61258

Fold-and-Go Booklet: To make a booklet, cut on the bold line. Fold along the thin horizontal line (keeping the programming to the outside) and then fold along the thin vertical line (keeping the cover to the outside). As you read each booklet page aloud, have each child color the appropriate picture on the page. For the final booklet page, explain to students that since we cannot see air, it is not necessary to color it.

Listen and Do

Draw.

Note to the teacher: Provide oral directions such as "Color a plant that usually grows in the desert" or "Circle a tree on which a sour fruit grows." Then specify what you would like the child to draw in the empty box, saying, for example, "Draw a plant that you see outside."

Plants

_____ knows
name

that plants

Class Book Page: Have a child write her name on a copy of the page and then write or dictate a response. If a child seems uncertain how to complete the prompt, suggest different verbs such as *are, need,* and *grow.* Then have her illustrate her work. Publish the pages in a class book titled "All About Plants!"

A Lovely Garden

Name _____

🖍 Color each plant.

Everything Science • ©The Mailbox® Books • TEC61258

Identifying plants

Name _____

Plenty of Plants

Cut.
Glue to match.

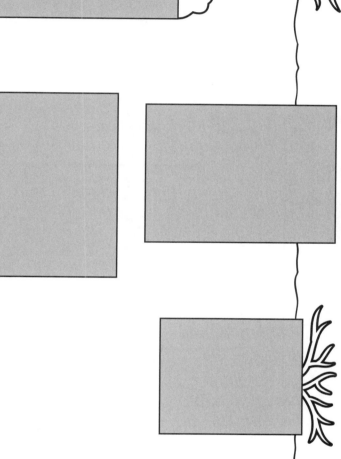

Everything Science • ©The Mailbox® Books • TEC61258

A Tall Flower

Cut.

Glue to match.

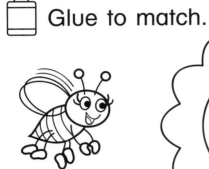

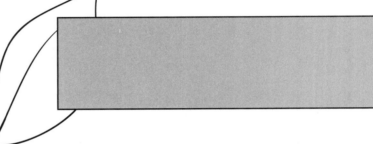

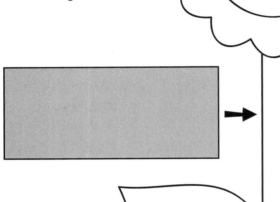

flower

roots

leaves

stem

Picture Cards: Set One
Page 100

How to Grow a Flower
by Morgan
1. Put a seed in the dirt.
2. Water it every day.
3. After a long time, a flower will grow!

Individual: Give each child an enlarged copy of the daisy card, a green pipe cleaner (stem), and a flowerpot cutout. Have the child color and cut out the daisy card. Then help her assemble the pieces so it looks like the flower is growing in the pot. On the pot have her write or dictate the steps for growing a flower.

Picture Cards: Set Two
Page 101

Individual: Give each youngster a copy of the page and a 9" x 12" sheet of construction paper. Have her cut apart the cards and glue each picture card to her paper. Then help her put glue along the top edge on the back of each word card and place the card atop the corresponding picture card to make a lift-the-flap page.

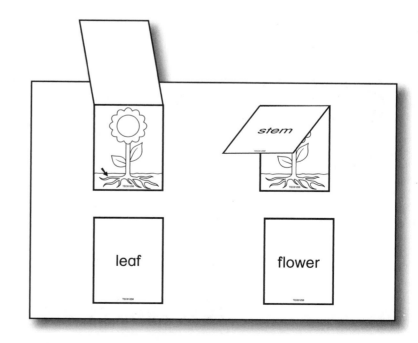

Bonus Activities
Plants

Fold-and-Go Booklet
Page 103

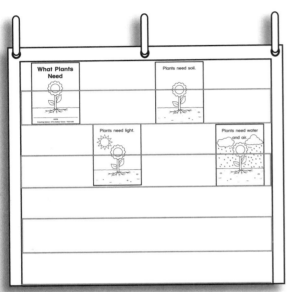

Whole group: Cut apart a copy of the page and display the resulting pictures in a pocket chart. Lead youngsters in singing the song shown. As you sing each verse, invite a child to find the appropriate picture.

What Plants Need
(sung to the tune of "Mary Had a Little Lamb")

Plants need things to help them grow, help them grow, help them grow.
Plants need things to help them grow. They need [the sun's bright light].

Continue with the following: *good, healthy soil; water and air.*

Class Book Page
Page 105

Individual: Complete the sentence starter on the page as shown; then copy the page to make a class supply. Give each child a programmed page. Have youngsters name different fruits that grow on plants. Ask each child to draw a picture of her favorite fruit on the page. Then help her label her illustration.

Plants

Stacey   knows
name

that plants can produce fruit that is good to eat!

Strawberry

Everything Science • ©The Mailbox® Books • TEC61258

Bugs

Picture Cards: Set One—Bugs

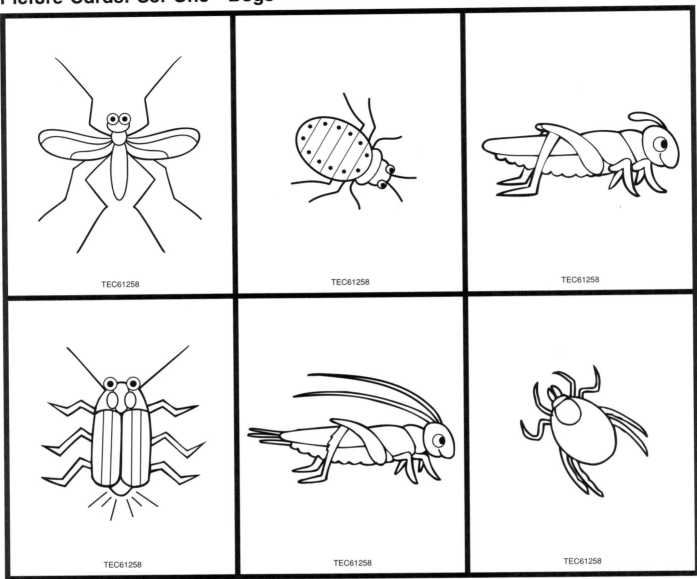

TEC61258

TEC61258

TEC61258

TEC61258

TEC61258

TEC61258

Distracter Cards

TEC61258

TEC61258

TEC61258

Picture Cards: Set Two—Flying Bugs and Crawling Bugs

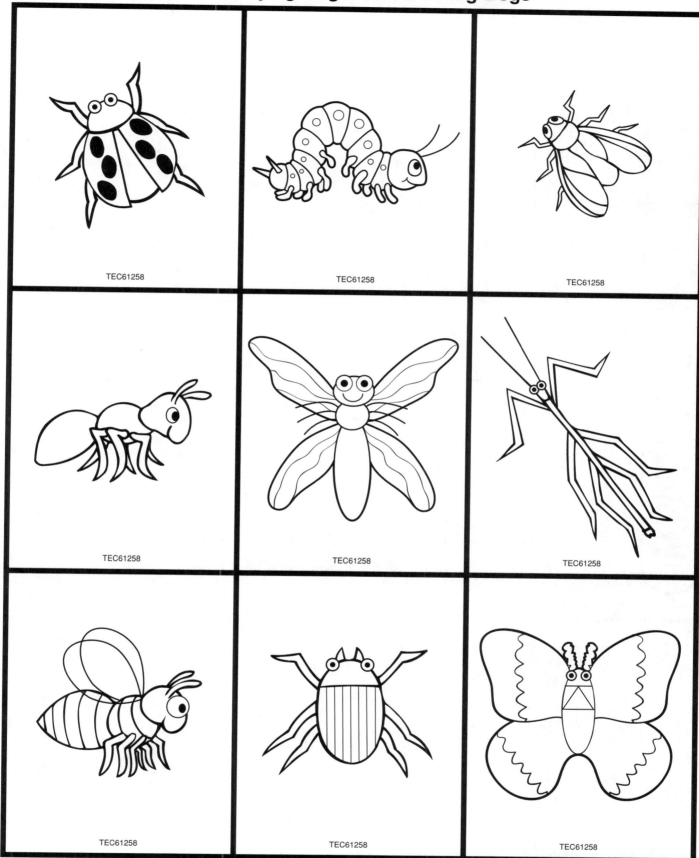

TEC61258

TEC61258

TEC61258

TEC61258

TEC61258

TEC61258

TEC61258

TEC61258

TEC61258

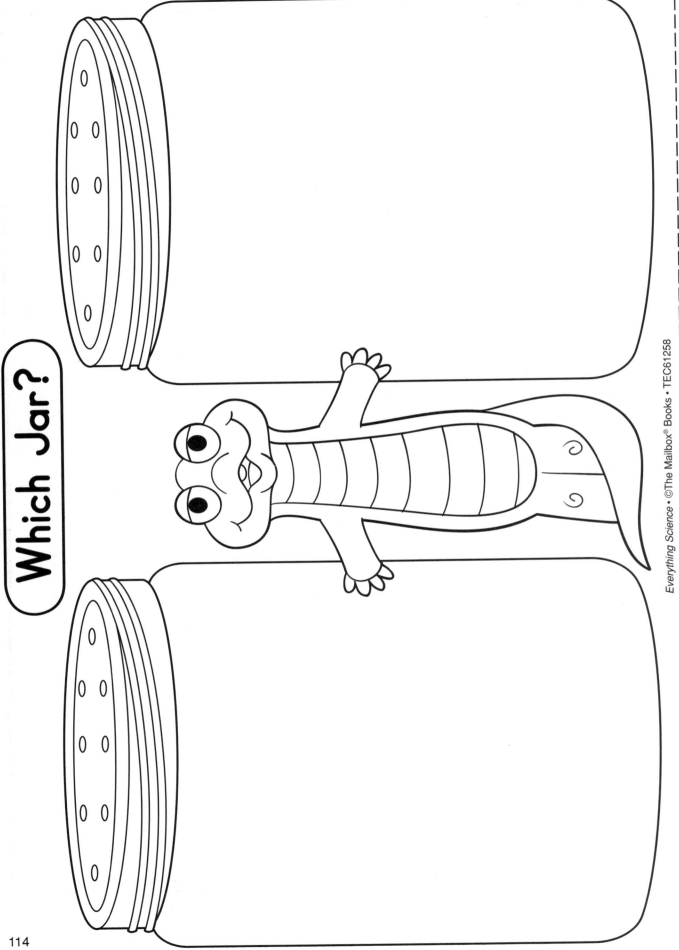

Which Jar?

Everything Science • ©The Mailbox® Books • TEC61258

Sorting Mat: Have students sort plastic bug manipulatives or sort the picture cards from pages 112 or 113. A student may also cut pictures of different bugs from magazines or other sources and sort them.

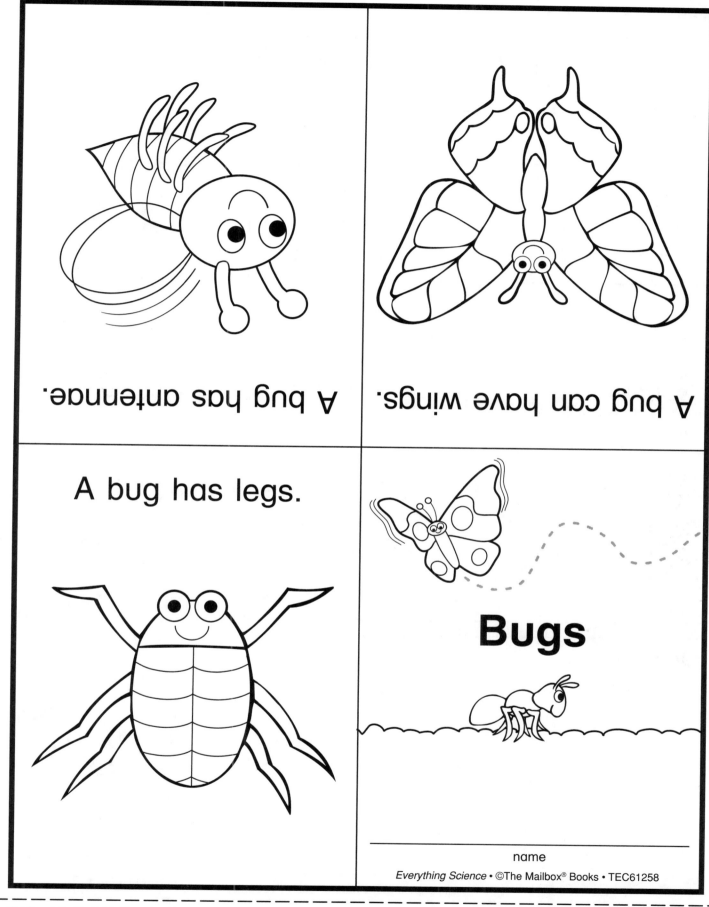

A bug has antennae.

A bug can have wings.

A bug has legs.

Bugs

name

Everything Science • ©The Mailbox® Books • TEC61258

Fold-and-Go Booklet: To make a booklet, cut on the bold line. Fold along the thin horizontal line (keeping the programming to the outside) and then fold along the thin vertical line (keeping the cover to the outside). As you read each booklet page aloud, have each child color the appropriate part of the bug on the page.

Listen and Do

Draw.

Bugs

_____ knows
name

that bugs

Class Book Page: Have a child write her name on a copy of the page and then dictate or write a response. If a child seems uncertain how to complete the prompt, suggest different verbs such as *are, need,* and *have.* Then have her illustrate her work. Publish the pages in a class book titled "We're Going Buggy!"

117

Buzzing Along

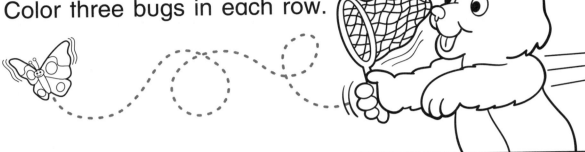

Color three bugs in each row.

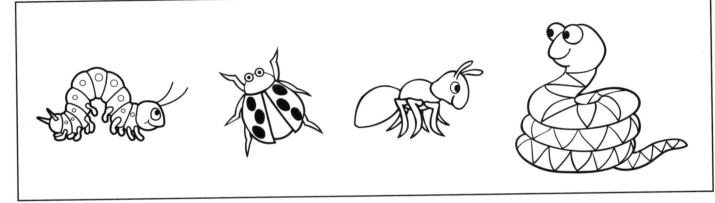

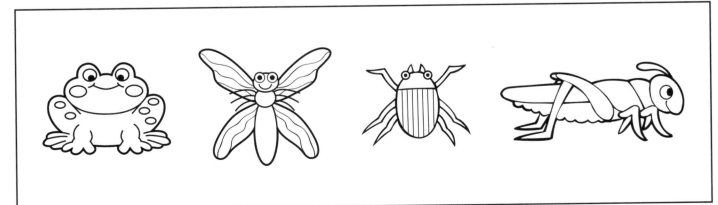

Everything Science • ©The Mailbox® Books • TEC61258

Name

Fly or Crawl?

Listen and do.

Everything Science • ©The Mailbox® Books • TEC61258

Note to the teacher: Have a child cut out the cards and glue in the sky each picture of a bug that flies and on the ground each picture of a bug that crawls.

A New Home

Cut.

Glue each bug in the jar.

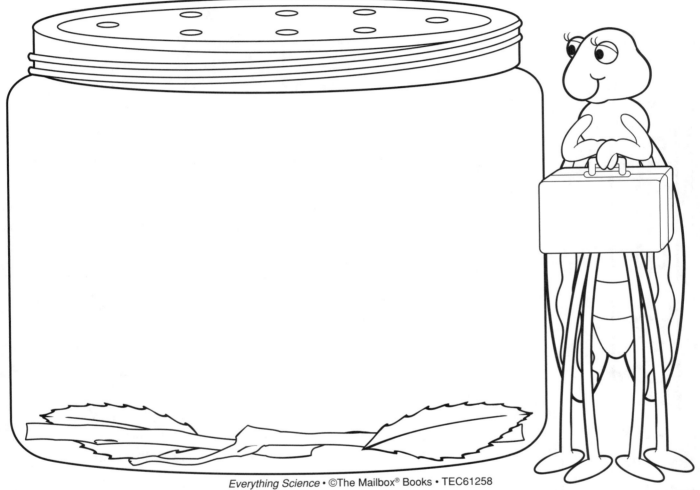

Everything Science • ©The Mailbox® Books • TEC61258

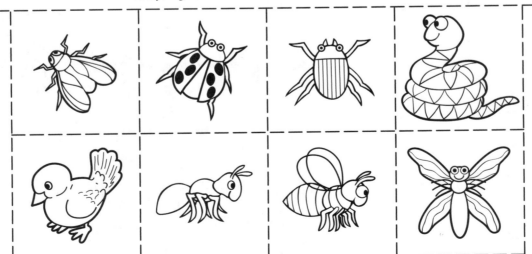

Picture Cards: Set One
Page 112

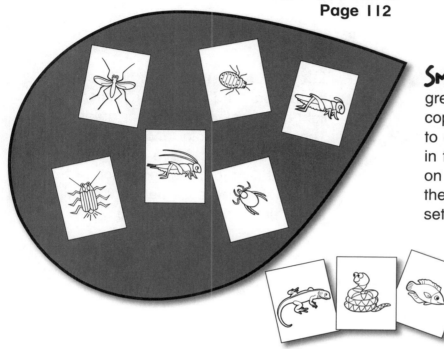

Small group: Cut out a large green tagboard leaf. Also cut out a copy of the cards and give one card to each child in the group. Each child, in turn, determines whether the item on his card is a bug. If it is, he places the card on the leaf. If it is not, he sets it aside.

Sorting Mat
Page 114

Center: Label a copy of the mat as shown. Place the mat at a center along with a supply of plastic bugs and plastic farm animals, mixed together. A child sorts each animal onto the appropriate side of the mat.

Picture Cards: Set Two
Page 113

Individual: Have each child color the bottom third of a 9" x 12" sheet of light blue construction paper green. Then have him color and cut out a copy of the cards. Have him glue each bug that flies to the blue portion of his paper (sky) and each bug that crawls to the green portion (ground).

Large group: Cut out a copy of the cards. Use some or all of the cards to make a graph, similar to the one shown, on a sheet of tagboard. Help each child personalize a sticky note and post it in the column representing his favorite bug. After each child has positioned his sticky note, discuss the results of the graph with the group. Incorporate the words *more, fewer, most, fewest,* and *equal* as appropriate.

Everything Science • ©The Mailbox® Books • TEC61258

Change and Growth

Everything Science • ©The Mailbox® Books • TEC61258

Note to the teacher: Ask each child to color the picture. As the child works, assess his prior knowledge by asking him to identify the young and old people and things in the picture and discuss how they changed.

Picture Cards: Set One—Change and Growth (Two Steps)

TEC61258

TEC61258

TEC61258

TEC61258

TEC61258

TEC61258

TEC61258

TEC61258

Everything Science • ©The Mailbox® Books • TEC61258

Picture Cards: Set Two—Change and Growth (Three Steps)

TEC61258

TEC61258

TEC61258

TEC61258

TEC61258

TEC61258

TEC61258

TEC61258

TEC61258

Time to Hatch!

Everything Science • ©The Mailbox® Books • TEC61258

Ordering Mat: Have students order picture cards from copies of pages 124 and 125. If students are ordering the two-step cards, place a manipulative over the third box on the mat so youngsters know that it is not needed.

Which One Changes and Grows?

name

Everything Science • ©The Mailbox® Books • TEC61258

Fold-and-Go Booklet: To make a booklet, cut on the bold line. Fold along the thin horizontal line (keeping the programming to the outside) and then fold along the thin vertical line (keeping the cover to the outside). Have each student circle on each page the pictured item that changes and grows.

Listen and Do

Draw.

Everything Science • ©The Mailbox® Books • TEC61258

Note to the teacher: Provide oral directions, such as "Color something that you eat that does not change and grow" or "Circle something that lives on a farm and changes and grows." Then specify what you would like the child to draw in the empty box, saying, for example, "Draw something that changes and grows."

Change and Growth

What things grow and change?

by _____
name

Class Book Page: Have a child write her name on a copy of the page and then dictate or write a response. If the child seems uncertain how to answer the question, suggest different objects that grow and change for her to choose from. Then have her illustrate her work. Publish the pages in a class book titled "Lots of Things Grow and Change."

What Changes and Grows?

Color the items that change and grow.

Everything Science • ©The Mailbox® Books • TEC61258

Name

Watch Me Grow!

✂ Cut.

Glue in order.

Everything Science • ©The Mailbox® Books • TEC61258

Bonus Activities
Change and Growth

Ordering Mat
Page 126

Individual: Give each child a copy of the ordering mat and help her think of something that grows and changes. Encourage her to draw a picture of the animal or plant as a baby in the left box. Have her draw it slightly older in the middle box and then fully grown in the final box.

"Listen and Do"
Page 128

Center: Cut apart the grid to make separate cards and attach the cards to labeled sorting sheets as shown. Then place the sorting sheets at a center along with a variety of magazines, scissors, and glue. A child searches through the magazines and finds pictures of items that do and do not change and grow. He cuts out the pictures and glues them to the appropriate sorting sheets.

Everything Science • ©The Mailbox® Books • TEC61258

Seasons

winter

spring

summer

fall

Note to the teacher: Ask a child to color the picture. As the child works, assess his prior knowledge by having him describe each season.

Picture Cards: Set One—Fall and Spring

Everything Science • ©The Mailbox® Books • TEC61258

Picture Cards: Set Two—Winter and Summer

TEC61258

TEC61258

TEC61258

TEC61258

TEC61258

TEC61258

TEC61258

TEC61258

TEC61258

Which Basket?

Everything Science • ©The Mailbox® Books • TEC61258

Sorting Mat: Have students sort small seasonal items into the baskets or have them sort the picture cards from pages 134 or 135.

winter

fall

spring

What's the Season?

summer

_____

name

Everything Science • ©The Mailbox® Books • TEC61258

Fold-and-Go Booklet: To make a booklet, cut on the bold line. Fold along the thin horizontal line (keeping the programming to the outside) and then fold along the thin vertical line (keeping the cover to the outside). To complete a booklet, a student colors the trees, adding details as needed, to correspond with the seasons.

Listen and Do

Draw.

Note to the teacher: Provide oral directions such as "Circle an item that can help you stay cool in the summer" or "Color something often found in trees in the spring." Then specify what you would like the child to draw in the empty box, saying, for example, "Draw something that sometimes falls from the sky during the winter."

Seasons

My favorite season is

_____ because

by _____
name

Class Book Page: Have a child write his name on a copy of the page and then dictate or write a response. If a child seems uncertain how to complete the prompt, review with him aspects of each season. Then have him illustrate his work. Publish the pages in a class book titled "Sensational Seasons."

Ready to Rake

 Color the pictures that show fall.

Name _____

Which Season?

✂ Cut.

🧴 Glue each picture to match.

☀ Summer

❄ Winter

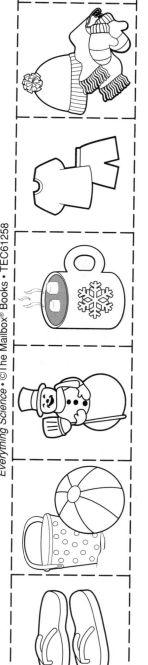

Everything Science • ©The Mailbox® Books • TEC61258

141

Name _____

142

🧴 Glue to match the season.

A Happy Hiker

Winter

Summer

Fall

Spring

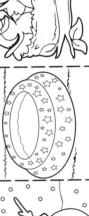

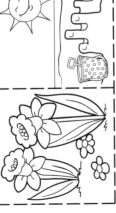

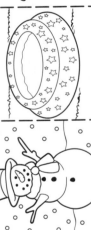

Bonus Activities
Seasons

Picture Cards
Pages 134 and 135

Center: Gather a variety of items that are associated with each of two different seasons. Label each of two containers with the name of the seasons and attach a corresponding picture card to each. Place the containers and items at a center. A child sorts each item into the appropriate container.

Individual: For each child, divide a sheet of paper into four sections and label each section with a different season as shown. Give each student one picture card to represent each season. Have her color each card and glue it in the appropriate section of her paper. Then help her draw arrows to show the cycle of the seasons.

Fold-and-Go Booklet
Page 137

In the spring there are lots of flowers. It is windy too.

Individual: Give each youngster one page of the booklet and have him complete and/or color the tree to match the season. Direct him to glue the booklet page to a sheet of paper and draw details to represent the season. Then have each child dictate a sentence or two to describe his seasonal scene.

Whole class: On a sheet of bulletin board paper, create a four-column graph like the one shown. Give each child a copy of a booklet page that shows her favorite season and have her complete and/or color the tree to match. Then have each child personalize her page. Next, in turn, help each child attach her page to the graph in the appropriate column. After the graph is complete, discuss the results with students.

Everything Science • ©The Mailbox® Books • TEC61258

Weather

Everything Science • ©The Mailbox® Books • TEC61258

Note to the teacher: Ask a child to color the picture. As the child works, assess his prior knowledge by having him discuss the items that are inappropriate for the pictured weather. Then have him name the type of weather in which each item would normally be used.

TEC61258

TEC61258

TEC61258

TEC61258

TEC61258

TEC61258

TEC61258

TEC61258

TEC61258

Everything Science • ©The Mailbox® Books • TEC61258

Picture Cards: Set Two—Hot Weather Items and Cold Weather Items

TEC61258

TEC61258

TEC61258

TEC61258

TEC61258

TEC61258

TEC61258

TEC61258

TEC61258

On a Cloud

148

Everything Science • ©The Mailbox® Books • TEC61258

Sorting Mat: Have students sort magazine pictures showing different kinds of weather, such as hot and cold or sunny and rainy, or have them sort the picture cards from pages 146 and 147.

¡oN

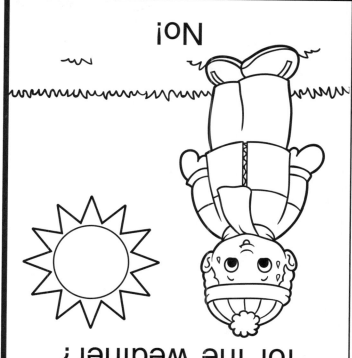

Is he dressed right for the weather?

¡oN

Is she dressed right for the weather?

Is she dressed right for the weather?

Yes!

What to Wear?

_____
name

Everything Science • ©The Mailbox® Books • TEC61258

Fold-and-Go Booklet: To make a booklet, cut on the bold line. Fold along the thin horizontal line (keeping the programming to the outside) and then fold along the thin vertical line (keeping the cover to the outside).

149

Name_____

Listen and Do

Draw.

Everything Science • ©The Mailbox® Books • TEC61258

Note to the teacher: Provide oral directions such as "Color a clothing item that can be used to keep your hands warm in cold weather" or "Circle an object that can protect your eyes from bright sunlight." Then specify what you would like the child to draw in the empty box by saying, for example, "Draw shoes that can be worn in hot weather."

Weather

The weather can be...

by _____
name

Class Book Page: Have a child write his name on a copy of the page and then dictate or write a response. If a child seems uncertain how to complete the prompt, suggest different types of weather, such as stormy, hot, or dangerous. Then have him illustrate his work. Publish the pages in a class book titled "Wild, Wonderful Weather!"

Name

Useful Items

Listen and do.

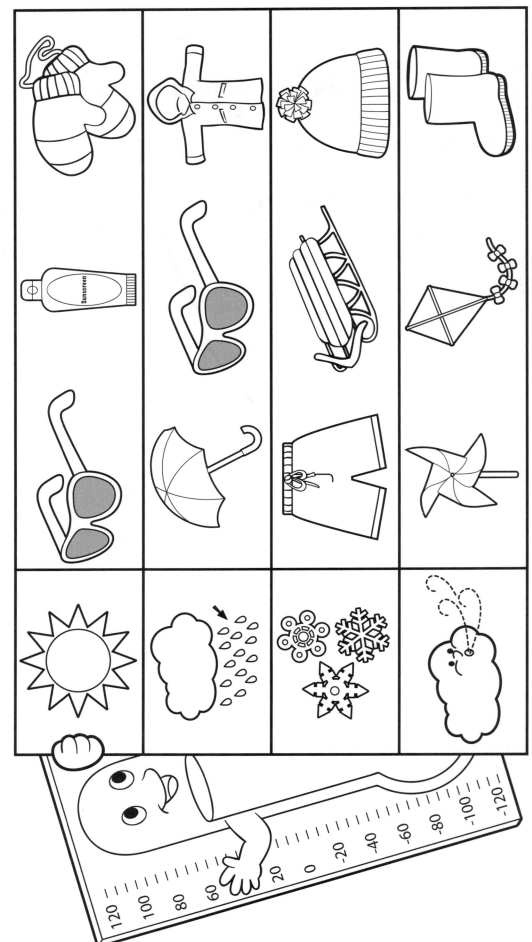

Everything Science • ©The Mailbox® Books • TEC61258

Note to the teacher: Direct each child to color the two items in each row that would most likely be used in the featured weather.

Name _____

Weather Watcher

✂ Cut.

🧴 Glue to match.

Splish, Splash!

✏️ Draw two examples of helpful weather.

✏️ Draw two examples of harmful weather.

Everything Science • ©The Mailbox® Books • TEC61258

Picture Cards: Set One
Page 146

When it is ☀
I like to...

Center: Program a sheet of blank paper with the sentence starter shown; then copy the page to make a class supply. Place the papers at a center along with cutout copies of the picture cards. A child glues a card to the sentence starter where indicated and draws a picture to complete the sentence.

Sorting Mat
Page 148

Individual: Give each child a copy of the sorting mat labeled with faces as shown. On the smiley face cloud, have him draw his favorite type of weather. Then, on the other cloud, have him draw the kind of weather he likes the least. Encourage each student to share and explain his drawings.

On a Cloud

Fold-and-Go Booklet
Page 149

Individual: Cut apart copies of the booklet so there is one page for each child. Each student glues his booklet page to another sheet of paper. If the pictured child's clothing matches the weather on the booklet page, the student draws on the paper other items that correspond with the weather. If the pictured child's clothing does not match the weather shown on the booklet page, she crosses out any items that do not match. Then she draws items that would be appropriate for use in the featured weather.

"Listen and Do"
Page 150

Whole Class: Have each student cut out the grid boxes from a copy of the page. Have him mix the cards and then help him glue them to another sheet of paper to make a lotto board. Cut apart a copy of the page for yourself to use as calling cards and give each student game markers. To play, take a card and announce the weather that is most associated with the pictured item. Each student covers an item on his board that could be used in that kind of weather. Play continues until a child has three markers in a row or column and announces, "Wonderful weather!"

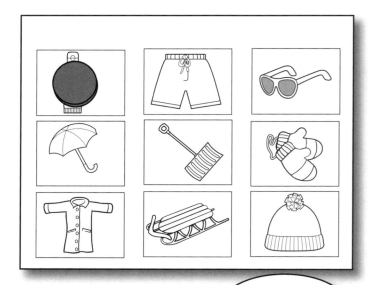

Cover a picture of something that could be used in sunny weather.

Rocks and Soil

Note to the teacher: Ask a child to color the picture. As the child works, assess her prior knowledge by asking her to name a picture on her paper of something that grows in soil *(tree)*. Then ask her to name a picture of something that lives in soil *(worms)* or digs a burrow under soil or rocks *(rabbit)*.

What else?

We make things out of **rocks.**

What else?

Soil helps things grow.

Some animals live in **soil.**

What else?

Rocks and Soil

name

Everything Science • ©The Mailbox® Books • TEC61258

Fold-and-Go Booklet: To make a booklet, cut on the bold line. Fold along the thin horizontal line (keeping the programming to the outside) and then fold along the thin vertical line (keeping the cover to the outside). Read each booklet page aloud and have students name other things that grow in soil, are made with rocks, and live in soil.

Listen and Do

Draw.

Everything Science • ©The Mailbox® Books • TEC61258

Note to the teacher: Provide oral directions, such as "Circle an animal that gives off a bad smell and lives in a burrow" or "Circle something that is built with rocks and that Humpty Dumpty sat on." Then specify what you would like the child to draw in the empty box, saying, for example, "Draw a picture of something that grows in soil."

Rocks and Soil

Soil is important because _____

_____.

We use rocks to _____

_____.

by _____
name

Name_____

Hungry for Berries

Follow the directions in each box.

Color 3 things that **grow** in soil.

Circle 3 animals that **live** in soil.

Cross off 2 things **not** made with rocks.

   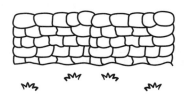

Soil Is Super!

✂ Cut.

🩹 Glue to match.

Does not live in soil:

Lives in soil:

Sky

Everything Science • ©The Mailbox® Books • TEC61258

Note to the teacher: Ask a child to color the picture. As the child works, assess his prior knowledge by asking him whether the pictures on his paper are of objects he would see in the sky during the day or at night. Encourage him to explain his answer.

At nighttime, I see…

In the daytime, I see…

Sometimes I see…

in the sky!

Sky

_____
name

Everything Science • ©The Mailbox® Books • TEC61258

Fold-and-Go Booklet: To make a booklet, cut on the bold line. Fold along the thin horizontal line (keeping the programming to the outside) and then fold along the thin vertical line (keeping the cover to the outside). To use the booklet, read each page aloud and have a child name the pictures on each page. On the second page, explain how the moon is mostly seen at night but is sometimes visible during the day.

Listen and Do

Draw.

Everything Science • ©The Mailbox® Books • TEC61258

Note to the teacher: Provide oral directions, such as "Circle an object whose name rhymes with *spoon* and that is seen in the sky mostly at night" or "Color a bright round object seen in the sky during the day." Then specify what you would like the child to draw in the empty box, saying, for example, "Draw a picture of something you have seen in the sky."

Sky

I see _____ in the sky during the day.

I see _____ in the sky at night.

by _____
name

Class Book Page: Have a child write his name on a copy of the page and then dictate or write a response. If a child seems uncertain how to complete the prompts, suggest different objects that can be seen in the sky during the day or at night for him to choose from. Then have him illustrate his work. Publish the pages in a class book titled "High in the Sky!"

Name_____

Can You See It?

Follow the directions in each box.

 Color 3 objects seen in the sky during the **day.**

 Color 2 objects seen in the sky at **night.**

 Cross off 2 objects **not usually** seen in the sky.

Day or Night?

Cut.

Sort.

Glue.

Day

Night

Caring for the Earth

Note to the teacher: Ask a child to color the picture. As the child works, assess her prior knowledge by having her discuss how the characters on the page are helping the earth.

Picture Cards: Caring for the Earth

Distracter Cards

Everything Science • ©The Mailbox® Books • TEC61258

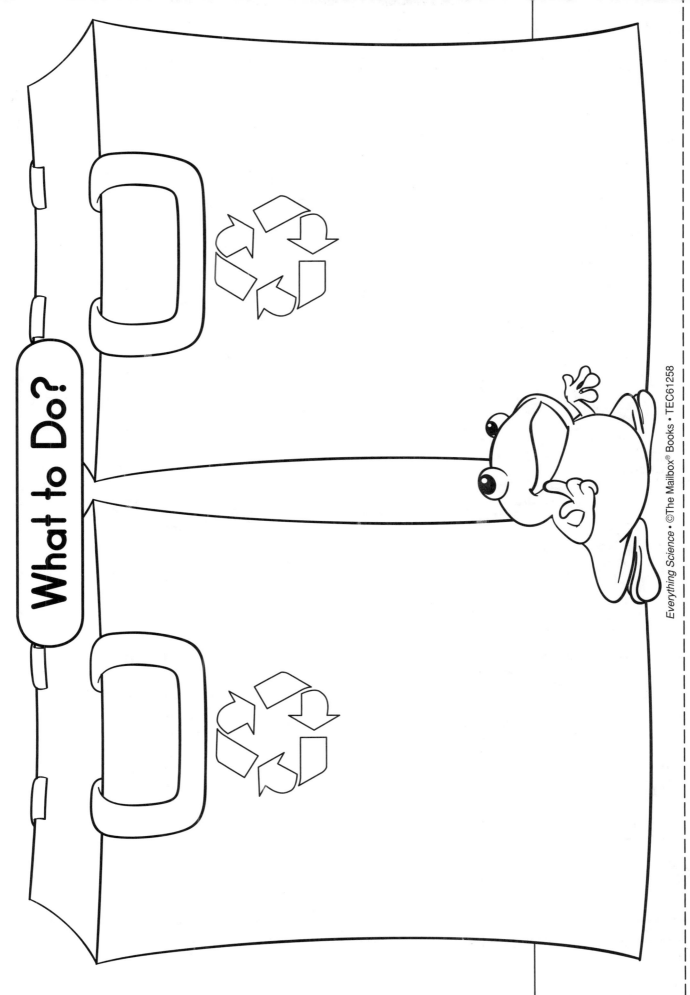

Everything Science • ©The Mailbox® Books • TEC61258

Sorting Mat: Have students sort magazine pictures of things that help or hurt the earth or have them sort the picture cards from page 170.

Turn off the water.

Plant a tree.

Reuse items.

Caring for the Earth

_____
name

Everything Science • ©The Mailbox® Books • TEC61258

Fold-and-Go Booklet: To make a booklet, cut on the bold line. Fold along the thin horizontal line (keeping the programming to the outside) and then fold along the thin vertical line (keeping the cover to the outside).

Listen and Do

Draw.

Note to the teacher: Provide oral directions such as "Cross out the picture of litter" or "Color the picture that shows where recyclable items should go." Then specify what you would like the child to draw in the empty box, saying, for example, "Draw something you can do to help the earth."

Caring for the Earth

To help the earth, I can…

by _____
name

Class Book Page: Have a child write his name on a copy of the page and then dictate or write a response. If a child seems uncertain how to complete the prompt, suggest different places where he can be helpful to the earth, such as at home, at the park, or at school. Then have him illustrate his work. Publish the pages in a class book titled "We Love Our Earth!"

Name_____

Good or Bad?

Cross out the picture in each row that shows something bad for the earth.

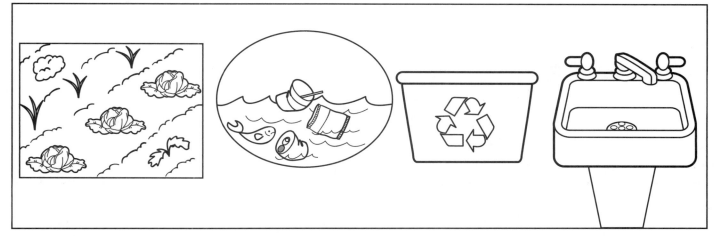

Name _____

A Clean Earth

✂ Cut.

Glue to show things that are good for the earth.

Everything Science • ©The Mailbox® Books • TEC61258